MICROHABITATS

# Life in a
# CAVE

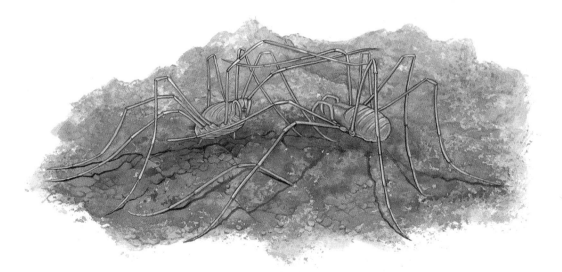

Clare Oliver

Evans

Evans Brothers Limited

First published in Great Britain in 2002 by Evans Brothers Limited
2A Portman Mansions
Chiltern Street
London W1U 6NR

Project Editors: Sean Dolan, Tamsin Osler, Louise John
Consultant: Michael Chinery
Production Director: Richard Johnson
Illustrated by Stuart Lafford
Designed by Ian Winton

Planned and produced by Discovery Books

British Library Cataloguing in Publication Data
Oliver, Clare
    Life in a cave - (Microhabitats)
    1. Cave animals - Juvenile literature
    I. Title
    578.7'584

    ISBN 0 237 52301 9

Printed in the United States

# Contents

# The Underground World

## The Cave

Caves are self-contained worlds, or **microhabitats**. The main types of caves are limestone caves, sea caves, ice caves and lava caves. Caves are cool, dark and often damp. These conditions do not suit every living thing, but some forms of life do well there. Plants cannot survive without sunlight, although mosses and ferns can grow in the shady entrance to the cave. Bacteria and fungi can also survive away from the light. They live on bat dung (sometimes called **guano**) and rotting leaves that blow into the cave.

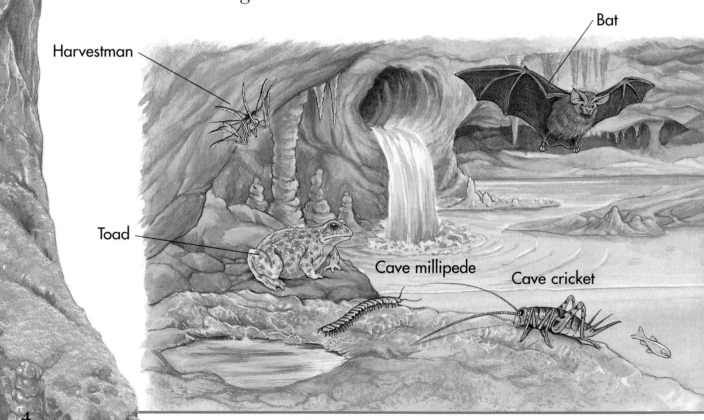

Harvestman

Bat

Toad

Cave millipede

Cave cricket

The cave gives many creatures a safe, quiet place to hide from predators. It offers protection from the weather and the temperature is the same throughout the year. Some creatures are so used to life in a cave that they never go outside. They are called **troglodytes**, from the Greek words meaning 'in a cave'.

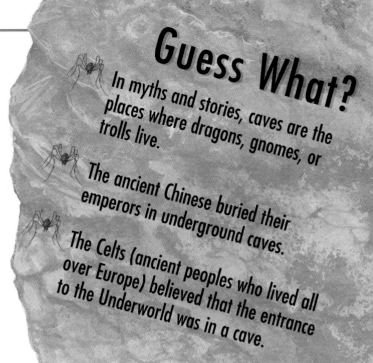

# Guess What?

In myths and stories, caves are the places where dragons, gnomes, or trolls live.

The ancient Chinese buried their emperors in underground caves.

The Celts (ancient peoples who lived all over Europe) believed that the entrance to the Underworld was in a cave.

Fungi

Brown rat

Cave fish

Flatworm

Cave beetle

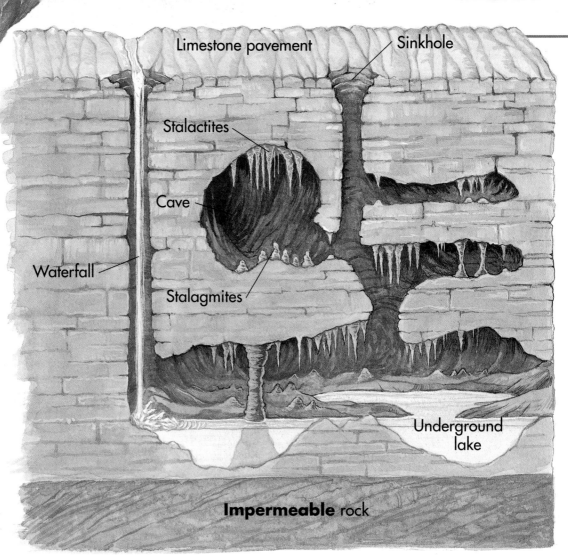

Limestone pavement • Sinkhole • Stalactites • Cave • Waterfall • Stalagmites • Underground lake • **Impermeable** rock

## How Caves Form

The most common type of cave is one that has formed in limestone rock, as above. Often, it is part of a whole system of caves linked by tunnels. Limestone rock is hard but it is also **soluble**. Over thousands of years, **acidic** surface water carves away at the rock, dissolving it to form channels, hollows and caves.

Caves often contain pillars made out of salt-like crystals. They are what is left behind when dripping water in the cave evaporates (turns into a gas or vapour).

Columns that hang down from the roof of the cave are called **stalactites**. Columns that grow up from the cave floor are called **stalagmites**.

This cave shows examples of both stalactites and stalagmites.

# See for Yourself

Take two plastic cups and fill them with water. Stir in lots of Epsom salts — as much as you can make dissolve in the water. Dip a length of string in the water then stretch it out between the two cups, with a saucer below the place where the string sags. Be patient! After four or five days, you will have your own stalactites and stalagmites.

# All Sorts of Caves

Limestone caves are only one type of cave. Sea caves form along the seashore where waves and stones wear away holes in the cliff. Waves can even make a hole in the roof of a sea cave. This is called a blowhole, and water squirts out of it as the waves rush into the cave at high tide.

A group of sea-lions take shelter in a cave as sea water rushes in.

Sea caves fill with swirling sea water twice a day, so few creatures are able to live there all the time. Only a few, such as barnacles and mussels, are able to cling to the slippery rock without being washed out to sea. Seaweed, crabs and fish can be swept into the cave and left stranded there between tides.

# Cold Caves

In the Arctic and Antarctic, ice caves form where icebergs are melted by warm sea water currents. These caves sometimes provide shelter for penguins or seals. Scientists have also learned that there are some microscopic life forms, such as fungi and algae, that can also survive in the freezing conditions.

Emperor penguins, found in Antarctica, have gathered near an ice cave formed by an iceberg.

# Slippery Swimmers

## Underground Rivers

Rivers and streams flow along dark tunnels deep inside cave networks. Many creatures live in this water range – from small flatworms and water snails, to newts, crayfish and fish. These animals make a **food chain**, with the smallest creatures living off rotting plants or animals in the water and then becoming food for larger **predators**.

The blind crayfish, like many cave-dwelling animals, is much paler than crayfish elsewhere.

## Eyeless Wonders

Creatures that live deep in the cave are usually pale and blind. They do not need sight because they live in total darkness. Instead, they use their other senses.

This cave fish has touch organs all over its body so that it can 'feel' its way around.

### Guess What?

The blind cave newt is pinkish-white, but it turns black if it is carried out into the sunlight.

Cave salamanders ooze a sticky substance from their skin. This allows them to walk up cave walls.

In 1999, scientists discovered a new type of eyeless crayfish in caves in Missouri, America.

## In and Out

Salamanders, like frogs and toads, are amphibians. In their adult form, they can move between the water and the cave floor, as long as they keep their slimy body moist. Some salamanders never leave the cave. Others, like the cave salamander, can live anywhere – as long as it is dark, damp and cavelike.

# Creepy-Crawlies

## Eight-Legged Monsters

The spiders that live in caves are hunters that chase prey rather than trap it in webs. Cave-dwelling spiders include wolf spiders and cellar spiders.

Wolf spiders have good eyesight and can move very quickly in pursuit of insects and other prey in the dim light of a cave.

In caves in America and many other parts of the world, you can also find scorpions. These night hunters thrive in the dark of the cave. They use the sting at the end of their tail to stun prey, such as spiders and insects.

Whip spiders and whip scorpions also live in caves. Both creatures have flat bodies and can slide into cracks to avoid predators.

Harvestmen are like spiders but they have very long legs with a tiny claw at the tip. They lurk at the cave mouth, where they hunt small insects.

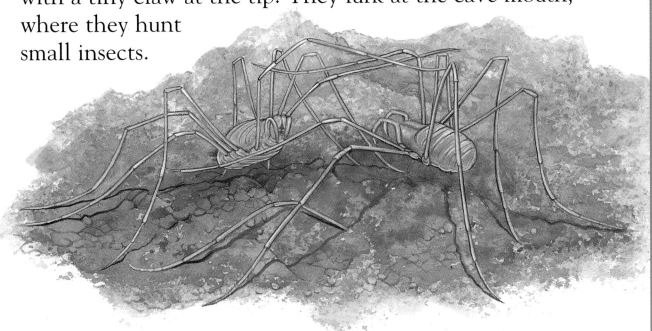

A male harvestman, or daddy longlegs, may bite off a leg of his opponent as they fight over a female.

## See for Yourself

This is what a spider's egg sack looks like. Many **arachnids**, including wolf spiders, carry their egg sacks to stop them from being eaten.

Next time you see a wolf spider, count how many eyes it has. The large ones are easy to spot, but what about the six smaller eyes?

## Lots of Legs

Also found scuttling about in the dark of the cave are unusual minibeasts known as myriapods, which means 'many-footed animals'. There are two main types: centipedes and millipedes. Both have huge numbers of legs and feet, but apart from that they are quite different.

## Fast Runners

Centipedes are fast-moving hunters. The most likely type to be found in a cave are scutigerids – short centipedes with 15 pairs of very long legs.

All centipedes use their claws, which more or less surround the head, to inject poison into their prey.

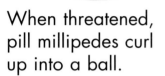

When threatened, pill millipedes curl up into a ball.

## Eating Leftovers

Millipedes are slow-moving vegetarians. Although there are no plants in caves, they find plenty to eat. The wind blows in leaves, bats drop seeds and millipedes even find bat dung tasty. Each time a millipede sheds its skin, it grows more segments – and even more legs!

Millipede means '1,000 legs', but no millipede has more than about 750.

## See for Yourself

Take a close look at a centipede. It has a pair of legs on each segment of its body.

Now, use a magnifying glass to look at a millipede. Millipedes have two pairs of legs on each of their body segments. Some millipedes have as many as 190 segments, others have only 13.

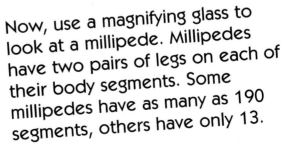

15

## Crickets and Beetles

Cave-dwelling insects include some types of crickets, beetles and strange creatures called rock crawlers. Cave crickets eat both plant and animal matter, dead or alive. Their long antennae, or feelers, help them to sense predators in the dark, as crickets are a good source of food for larger animals.

Cave crickets, like this one, sleep in the cave, but leave it each night to scavenge for food.

## Dead Meat

Rock crawlers, also known as grylloblattids, look a bit like earwigs, with very small eyes or even none at all. Because they do not rely on sight, it does not matter to them whether it is night or day. Rock crawlers are **scavengers** that search for dead creatures to eat. They also eat slow-moving prey.

## Guess What?

Only 25 kinds of rock crawler are known. They all live in the mountains in Asia and North America.

Rock crawlers take five years to develop into proper adults.

Some species of beetles exist only in one or a few caves. The Tooth Cave beetle, for instance, is only found in caves in Texas, America.

Many different types of beetles visit caves, but only a few live there all the time. Cave-dwelling beetles are often eyeless. Some eyeless cave beetles feed solely on cricket eggs and their larvae.

Eyeless beetles depend on a sharp sense of smell to find their food.

## Mites and Parasites

Bat dung, or guano, is a rich food for many different life forms. Blind springtails, bristletails, and silverfish eat their way through the rotting dung. Adapted to life in a cave, these primitive small, wingless insects have soft, pale bodies. They are also found on fungi and other **organic** matter in the cave.

The springtail is named for its tail. When not in use, its tail is folded under its stomach. By flicking the tail downwards, the insect can catapult itself through the air.

In the cave, as in all habitats, all creatures live off other living things in some way. However, fleas, and ticks are true parasites because they feed on others without killing them. For example, bat fleas often make a tasty meal of the bats' blood.

Bat flies are among the most unusual creatures found in a cave. Despite their name, adult bat flies have no wings. The female bat fly keeps her eggs inside her body – and also the young **larvae**, when they hatch.

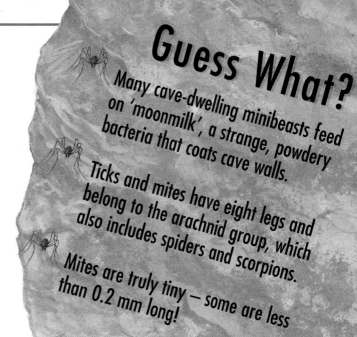

**Guess What?**

Many cave-dwelling minibeasts feed on 'moonmilk', a strange, powdery bacteria that coats cave walls.

Ticks and mites have eight legs and belong to the arachnid group, which also includes spiders and scorpions.

Mites are truly tiny – some are less than 0.2 mm long!

An adult bat fly.

As the larva develops, it turns into a **pupa**, a sort of sleeping state, and the mother bat fly lays the pupa on the wall of the bat roost. An adult bat fly only comes out from this pupa state when it senses a bat nearby. It climbs onto the bat and takes its first drink of blood!

**Thirsty ticks**

Ticks can suck up more than their own body weight in blood. They swell to several times their normal weight!

Before feeding

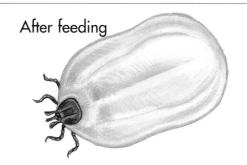

After feeding

# A Place to Sleep

## Roosting Bats

Bats are probably the best-known cave dwellers. During the daytime, cool, damp caves are an ideal place for roosting bats.

Some bats are solitary, which means that they live alone. Others nest together in enormous colonies. Some bats live in the cave throughout the year, while others go there for just one season, either to nest or **hibernate.** Different types of bats may even roost in the same cave.

A horseshoe bat hibernates by hanging upside down from a rock. Both the greater and the lesser horseshoe bat like to live in caves.

## Batty Effects

The presence of large bat colonies in a cave can alter the microhabitat. Their body heat can raise the cave temperature to about 100° Fahrenheit (38° Celsius). Bats breathe in oxygen and breathe out carbon dioxide. The level of carbon dioxide, together with ammonia (a poisonous gas produced by the bat dung) reduces the amount of oxygen in the cave. This means there is a limit to the number of bats and other mammals that can live there.

As dusk falls, bats wake from their daytime roost and prepare to leave the cave in search of food.

## Guess What?

All bats are legally protected in the UK and most other European countries.

The Alabama cave fish survives in just one cave, under one bat roost. If that bat colony were lost, the cave fish would become extinct.

## Bats on the Hunt

Bats are nocturnal animals – they sleep by day and hunt by night. They have a highly developed method for finding insect prey. It is called **echolocation**. The bats make short, high-pitched squeaks and when their squeaks hit objects, such as moths, these sounds bounce back to the bats as echoes. From these echoes, which are not **audible** to humans, bats can navigate and find prey in the dark.

The horseshoe bat preys on flies, beetles, spiders and moths.

## Finding a Meal

1. The bat sends out high-pitched squeaks that travel as sound waves.

2. The squeaks bounce back off a moth as an echo.

3. From the echo, the bat can pinpoint where the moth is.

## Mothy Meals

Because it takes a lot of energy to fly, bats eat all the time when they are awake. In one night, a large colony of 10 million free-tailed bats can eat 100 tons of insects! Moths are common prey, mainly because they are night-fliers, too. In tropical regions, there are **species** of bats that feed on fruit, frogs, or even fish.

## Bat Nurseries

Sometimes, bats fly to a particular cave to give birth. Each year, for example, around 10 million Mexican free-tailed bats travel more than 1,200 km to reach Bracken Cave in Texas, America. Each bat gives birth to a single baby.

This cave in New Mexico, is known as 'The Bat Cave'. Each summer millions of bats roost there.

## Hide and Seek

Bat mothers do not carry their young with them when they go out hunting. Instead, they leave their young behind and fly back throughout the night to feed them milk. There can be millions of young bats in a 'nursery', but a mother finds her own baby easily. Even if it has moved from where she left it, she can recognise its call and its scent.

Bats are mammals, which means they give birth to live young that feed on their mother's milk.

25

## Cave Visitors

Bats are not the only mammals that seek shelter in a cave. Other mammal visitors include mice, rats, foxes and wolves. In some countries, brown and black bears shelter in caves, especially during the winter months when they live off the fat they have stored in their bodies. Unlike hedgehogs and bats, bears do not truly hibernate. They wake from time to time to eat, and their heart rate and breathing does not slow down as in other hibernating animals.

## Sneaky Predators

Birds and reptiles will venture into the mouth of a cave to escape the winter winds. Vultures, owls and snakes are also tempted in by the hope of a meal — perhaps of a young bat!

## Guess What?

Many thousands of years ago, people sometimes lived in caves, too. They left behind some of the earliest known works of art. Cave wall paintings of animals at Lascaux, in France, are 20,000 years old.

Caves in Missouri, America, contain the remains of prehistoric animals, including sabre-toothed tigers.

Some creatures become accidental visitors to caves, falling in through a hole in the ground above the cave.

All of these visitors add to the cave microhabitat. Their dung, fur or feathers will provide food or shelter for minibeasts and other small creatures.

Barn owls may feed on snails, as well as on mice, frogs and voles.

# Caves Around the World

## Amazing Cave Dwellers

Caves are found all over the world. Their inhabitants differ from region to region. Sometimes, animals are unique to one particular cave. Endangered eyeless catfish are found only in a handful of Mexican caves, for example.

Tropical rainforest caves provide a home to wide variety of animal life, including some unusual birds and bats.

Oilbirds are most commonly found in tropical regions of South and Central America.

## Flying High

Some of the most unusual cave dwellers are birds that use echolocation, in the way that bats do. Oilbirds use echolocation and so do the cave swifts of Asia and Australia. Flying foxes and other fruit bats also live in tropical caves. These bats rely more on sight than echolocation to find their sugary foods of fruit or flowers. Their dung provides food for cave cockroaches.

## Guess What?

The larvae of fungus gnats, which live in caves in New Zealand and Australia, glow in the dark. They use sticky threads hung from the rocks to trap flying insects!

The saliva or spit produced by a cave swift to cement its nest is considered a delicacy (a rare and tasty food) by some people. They risk their lives to collect the nests, from which they make birds' nest soup.

# Glossary

**Acidic**  Containing a high level of acid.

**Arachnids**  A group of arthropods, or invertebrates, that have eight jointed legs. Arachnids include spiders, scorpions, ticks and mites.

**Audible**  A sound that is loud enough to be heard.

**Echolocation**  Using the echoes of sound waves to navigate and find prey.

**Food chain**  Links between plants and animals in a microhabitat that reflects the way energy, in the form of food, passes from one species of organism to another.

**Guano**  The droppings of bats or seabirds.

**Hibernation**  A very deep sleep that helps some animals to survive the winter.

**Impermeable**  When a material does not allow fluids to pass through it.

**Larvae**  The young form of an insect, which looks different from the adult.

**Microhabitat**  A small, specialised place, such as a tide pool or freshwater pond, where particular animals and plants live and grow.

**Organic**  Plant or animal matter.

**Predator**  An animal that hunts other animals for food.

**Pupa**  The stage in an insect's life when the larva changes into an adult.

**Scavenger**  An animal or organism that eats, or otherwise uses, waste materials, such as decaying animal bodies.

**Soluble**  Able to be dissolved, like sugar dissolves in coffee.

**Species**  A specific type of animal or plant.

**Stalactites**  Rock formations that hang down from the ceiling of a cave. They occur in places where limestone-rich water that has seeped out of the rock collects and drips to the cave floor.

**Stalagmites**  Rock formations that grow up in column form from the floor of a cave. Stalagmites form where water drips down from the ceiling of the cave.

**Troglodyte**  A cave dweller.

# Acknowledgements

The publishers would like to thank the following for permission to reproduce their pictures:
Front Cover: E. & D. Hosking/FLPA; p.7: Haroldo Palo, Jr./NHPA; p.8: David Hosking/FLPA; p.9: Mark Jones/Oxford Scientific Films; p.10: David M. Dennis/Oxford Scientific Films; p.11: Max Gibbs/Oxford Scientific Films; p.12: Joe McDonald/Bruce Coleman; p.15: Michael Tweedie/NHPA; p.16: L. Lee Rue/FLPA; p.17: Daniel Heuclin/NHPA; p.20: E. & D. Hosking/FLPA; p.21: J.A.L. Cooke/Oxford Scientific Films; p.22: E. & D. Hosking/FLPA; p.24: Stephen Dalton/NHPA; p.25: Mantis Wildlife Films/Oxford Scientific Films; p.26: Terry Whittaker/FLPA; p.27: Fritz Polking/FLPA; p.28: Mark Newman/FLPA; p.29: Jargon & Christine Sohns/FLPA.

# Index